Roman Catholicism

Peter Kelly

Ward Lock Educational

ISBN 0 7062 3601 7

First published 1971
Reprinted 1973

Set in 11 on 12 point Press Roman medium on an IBM 72 Composer
by David Ashley Limited
for Ward Lock Educational
116 Baker Street, London W1M 2BB
Printed in Spain

Contents

Acknowledgments

The author and publishers would like to thank the following for their help in supplying the photographs and drawings which illustrate this book:Father Martin Bennett p 41; Elizabeth Clarke p 11; Concordia Films, London pp 22,33,35 (taken from the filmstrip *Roman Catholicism*); John Hayes pp 8,21,22,23,24, 26,29,34,42; Manning Photographers p 27; The Trustees of the National Gallery, London p 6; Paul Popper pp 12,13,15,40,43; The Trustees of the Tate Gallery, London pp 7,18,39. In particular we would like to thank Father Martin Bennett who gave us so much help with the manuscript and illustrations.

1 Introduction

The Creed

The twelve articles which form the basis of Roman Catholic belief, and which the Roman Catholic believes have been revealed by God, are contained in the Apostles' Creed which has been used since the early days of Christianity:

I believe in God the Father Almighty, Maker of Heaven
and Earth: And in Jesus Christ His only Son our Lord,
Who was conceived by the Holy Ghost, Born of the
Virgin Mary, Suffered under Pontius Pilate, Was crucified,
dead, and buried. He descended into hell: The third day
he rose again from the dead: He ascended into heaven,
And sitteth on the right hand of God the Father
Almighty. From thence he shall come to judge the living
and the dead. I believe in the Holy Ghost, the Holy
Catholic Church, the Communion of Saints, the
forgiveness of sins, the resurrection of the body, and
the life everlasting. Amen.

You may not really understand what some of the articles in the Creed mean. They will be explained as we go along.

The Nicene Creed, which is recited at the Mass, is longer and expresses the same beliefs more fully. In addition to the contents of the Creeds, Catholics also believe all the other truths which are found in Scripture and in Tradition.

God

Most people in previous ages have attributed the natural laws which govern the world, the existence of the world and the life that inhabits it, to the work of a supreme being whom we call God. The basic difference among people who accept the existence of God lies in their interpretation of the relationship that exists between God and the world, and in particular, man. The Catholic learns, as far as it is

Piero della Francesca, a fifteenth century Italian artist, set his painting of
The Nativity against the background of his native Italian countryside.

humanly possible, of God's relationship with the world and of his own
with God, how he can deepen, strengthen or even sever it, from what
God has revealed in the teachings of Jesus Christ as contained in the
Bible and the teachings of the Church to which he belongs which was
founded by Christ. I say humanly possible because it is impossible
for men to form a complete idea of a being infinitely intelligent,
powerful, wise and good.

The Catholic Church does advance proofs for the existence of God,
but we should remember that proof is related to knowledge, not belief.
Belief in God, or faith as it is called, is a gift, a power that comes from
God. It cannot come simply as the conclusion of a process of reasoning,
although this may be the means by which God gives a person the gift
of faith.

Jesus Christ

Christ was a Jew born in Palestine during the period of Roman
occupation a little less than 2000 years ago. He came of a poor
family and spent the greater part of his life in an out of the way

**Christ in the House of His Parents by John Everett Millais. Joseph, Jesus's
stepfather, was a carpenter.**

village called Nazareth in the province of Galilee. The last three years
of his life were spent travelling about the country preaching and
working miracles. He incurred the enmity of the Sanhedrin, the
presiding Council of the Jewish religion, because of his religious claims
and teaching, and was handed over to the Roman authorities to be
tried as a political dissenter. He was sentenced first to be flogged and
then to be executed by being nailed hand and foot to two pieces of
wood joined in the form of a cross. On the third day after his burial
he performed the greatest of his miracles by returning to life. He
presented himself to his disciples on several occasions before finally
taking leave of them and ascending into heaven.

**The twelfth of the
Fourteen Stations
of the Cross (see
page 42) portrays
Jesus dying on
the cross.**

The Holy Trinity

To Catholics, as indeed to most Christians, Christ was not just a
prophet, not simply a divine representative, a holy or inspired man,
but God Himself, the second person of the Holy Trinity, the Godhead
that is composed of three Persons: the Father, the Son and the Holy
Spirit. This is a mystery, a matter that surpasses human understanding,
a truth revealed by Christ, a claim substantiated by his miracles, his
teachings and the prophecies of his Jewish predecessors.

The Bible

Our knowledge of Christ's life and teaching comes from the second
part of a collection of writings known as the Scriptures or the Bible.
By far the greater part of the Bible, the Old Testament, is an account
of God's dealings with the Jewish people from the earliest times.
It contains many prophecies of Christ's birth, life, death and
resurrection. The small section, the New Testament, is an account of
the life and teaching of Christ, and of some of his closest followers in
the period following his departure from this world. Consisting of the
four Gospels, the Acts of the Apostles, and the Epistles, it is of even
greater importance to the Christian, Catholic or otherwise, than the
Old Testament, for in addition to altering certain of the old laws
given by God to the Jewish people, Christ instituted a new law which
was to apply to all men. Although the Bible has many authors, Christians
of every denomination are united in believing that its contents were
directly inspired by God.

Tradition

The Apostles handed on to the Church the full teaching of Christ. Christ
commanded them to teach all he had entrusted to them. Some of this
teaching is contained in the inspired books of the New Testament. The
remainder was handed on in other ways, such as by word of mouth or
preaching. This latter we call Tradition.

2   The founding of the Catholic Church

The Catholic believes that the Catholic Church was founded by Jesus Christ, the human incarnation of God, and that other Christian Churches are to a greater or lesser extent a departure from the path laid down by Christ for those who believed in him and his message.

The four marks
The Catholic claims that Christ, during his lifetime, founded a Church and that this Church was possessed of four distinguishing characteristics or marks — universality, apostolicity, unity and holiness. In this chapter we shall examine these marks and show how the Catholic sees them as having always been and continuing to be identical with those of the Church to which he adheres.

Universality
At the beginning of his public life, Christ selected from among those who listened to his teaching, twelve men — ordinary working people — whom he asked to give up their livelihood, their families and their homes to follow him. They were to be trained to carry on the work of teaching and conversion after he had left them. They were not to restrict their activities to the country of their birth, to men of their own or neighbouring nationality, but were to split up and to travel to all parts of the world, preaching God's message to all men, of all colours and of all nationalities: 'Go ye into the whole world and preach the gospel to every creature ' (Mark 16: 15).

The word 'catholic' means universal. For the past two thousand years the Catholic Church has been putting into effect this injunction of its founder. Men and women who are prepared to sacrifice all the pleasures and comforts of normal existence, who are willing, when called upon, to make the supreme sacrifice of their own lives, have been sent to every part of the globe. The presence of Catholic communities today in almost if not every country is a living testimony of the Church's universality or catholicity. However much one may disagree with the tenets of the Catholic Church one cannot dispute the aptness of its name.

Apostolicity

From among the twelve men he chose as his first Apostles, Christ
singled out one as their leader to whom he gave special powers:
'And I say to thee: That thou are Peter; and upon this rock I
will build my church. ... And I will give to thee the keys of the
kingdom of heaven. And whatsoever thou shalt bind upon earth,
it shall be bound also in heaven: and whatsoever thou shalt loose
on earth, it shall be loosed also in heaven ' (Matthew 16: 18-19).
Christ also gave authority to the other Apostles: 'As the Father
hath sent me, I also send you ' (John 20: 21). 'He that heareth
you, heareth me: and he that despiseth you, despiseth me '
(Luke 10: 16).

St Peter

The Catholic understands that this authority given to the Apostles
did not make them independent of each other; they were a united
body of men with Peter as their head. Their authority and that of

The world-famous St Peter's church in Rome, beneath which St Peter is buried.

Peter was to be transmitted by them to their appointed successors who would in turn pass on this authority. The Pope and the bishops of the Church are considered to be the legitimate successors of the Apostles, and this is what the Catholic means when he claims that his Church is apostolic.

Priests, who constitute the third rank in the hierarchy of the Church, are men appointed by bishops as their helpers, but they do not form part of the apostolic succession. Of them more will be said later.

Peter became the first bishop of Rome and was crucified there. This will explain why Rome has remained, with little interruption, the centre of the Catholic Church and the residence of the popes who succeeded Peter.

Papal and Episcopal Authority

The function of the Pope, or the Holy Father as he is respectfully
referred to by Catholics, together with that of the bishops, needs
to be clearly understood as it has been basically a refusal to accept
the legitimacy of the authority of the Apostles' successors that has
led to the creation of so many other Christian Churches. Whereas
most Protestants, i.e. non-Catholic Christians, believe that God
enlightens the mind of each person who sincerely endeavours to
understand the Scriptures, the Catholic accepts that God
the Holy Spirit guides the Pope and the bishops in their
teaching and preserves them from error when they pronounce
unanimously and solemnly on certain fundamental issues. This does
not mean that the Catholic does not or is not encouraged to read
the Scriptures, but he feels that if their basic interpretation by
individual men is to avoid contradiction then it is through Christ's
appointed representative on earth that the answer must come.

Pope Paul VI

13

Very seldom is the Pope called upon to exercise his special power;
once or perhaps twice during the course of a century does he speak
'infallibly', that is, without error. The infallibility of the Pope has been
much misunderstood; it has often been associated with the idea of the
Pope being able to do no wrong. We have indisputable historical
evidence that a small handful of popes led very worldly lives, but
this should in no way shake the belief of the true Catholic, any more
than the occasional confrontation with an unworthy priest, for if God
could take human form, live as a poor, working class man, allow
Himself to be spat upon and put to death by His own creatures, then
surely He can work through unworthy people and in so doing make
men appreciate all the more His great love for them?

Recently the present Pope, Paul VI, has condemned artificial
methods of birth control and, in so doing, has reaffirmed the teaching
of his predecessors. As yet there has been no infallible, *ex cathedra*
pronouncement. Perhaps there will not be. But the Catholic, bearing
in mind the guiding presence of the Holy Spirit among those vested
with apostolic authority and at the same time the limitations and
inadequacies of his own understanding, must realize that if his own
views on birth control differ then he is bound to give the deepest
respect and consideration to such a pronouncement and endeavour
to bring his thinking in line with that of the Church.

Unity

On the night before his death Christ prayed: '... not for them
only (i.e. the Apostles) do I pray, but for them also who through
their word shall believe in me: that they may all be one, as thou,
Father, in me, and I in thee; that they also may be one in us:
that the world may believe that thou hast sent me '
(John 17: 20-21).

Christ desired for his Church an absolute unity, a unity which
should exclude all division. This is probably the most fundamental
characteristic of Christ's Church. Time and again the Apostle Paul
compares the Church to a living body. He sees the members of the
Church as parts of the same living organism. Vivified by the same
spiritual life, they should believe the same doctrine, participate in
the same worship, and yield obedience to one and the same authority.

Within the Catholic Church there is unity of government; all its
members are bound by the same beliefs and all observe the same forms
of worship. The sacrifice of the Mass is the focal point of Catholic
worship and, allowing for differences of ceremonial and custom, is the .

The Second Vatican Council summoned by Pope John XXIII in 1962 to update the Church. Over 2,500 bishops from all over the world attended.

same everywhere. Together with the sacraments, it is the source of spiritual life that gives to the Church its real unity as we shall see later.

It cannot be denied that there is and there has always been a degree of disunity within the Church, caused by the badness, the weakness, the misguidedness or simply the lack of faith of some of its members. It could also be considered a contributory factor in the emergence of so many other Christian Churches. One must, however, realize that the prayer of Christ was dependent on the good will and free choice of mankind, and the kind of unity he envisaged can never be fully achieved in this world.

Holiness

Christ commanded his followers to aim at perfection: they were to be perfect as their heavenly Father was perfect. This was to be their supreme aim in life and that of everyone who believed in him. Perfection or holiness is the Christian ideal.

The Catholic attains holiness through observance of the teachings of Christ as contained in the Scriptures and as interpreted by his apostolic representatives on earth, but observance in itself does not constitute holiness or Christian perfection. Holiness means being close to God; it means increasing the presence of God within oneself. Christ, as the incarnation of God, was the personification of holiness, and the closer one comes to Christ, the holier one becomes. The Apostles were able to attain perfection because they were filled with the Holy Spirit and the love of Christ. We shall see shortly, when we come to examine what the Catholic believes, the way in which Christ and the Holy Spirit make themselves present to every member of the Church, and how this presence gives to the Catholic Church its basic holiness and unity.

The greatest sign of the Church's holiness is to be found in the lives of the saints.

Saints

Just as the Apostles observed to a supreme degree the teachings of Christ, there have always been people within the Catholic Church who have done likewise, who have, as an expression of their love for their creator, abandoned all those things that most men work and live for and dedicated their lives entirely to God. There have been many too who have attained sanctity, by which we mean a high degree of holiness, by living very humdrum, ordinary, family lives, yet at the same time maintaining a complete detachment from earthly possessions. And there are the martyrs, those who gave their lives rather than renounce their beliefs.

The ninth article of the Apostles' Creed contains the phrase 'the Communion of Saints'. 'Saints' in this instance means something rather different from the explanation given above. In addition to the living members of the Church there are those who are dead, whether in heaven or purgatory, and who are, to a greater or lesser extent, in union with Christ. All members of the Church in heaven, on earth, in purgatory, constitute the communion of saints.

3   What Catholics believe

Suffering
If there is a God and He loves His creatures, as Christians claim, then how is it that He tolerates so much unmerited suffering? How is it that little children are allowed to die in agony, that innocent people become the victims of injustice and oppression? The problem of suffering is the greatest of human problems, and for the Christian it can only be answered in terms of the suffering of Christ. God, by becoming man, by experiencing the day to day hardships of mankind, by suffering bereavement, loneliness, the tortures and agony of a terrible death, has given a value and a meaning to all suffering in all ages by all people.

But why the need for suffering in the first place? Why should Christ have to suffer, why should anyone have to suffer? To answer this question, we must go back in time to the first man and woman, and we must understand the notion of sin.

Sin
Whether the story in the Old Testament of the first man and woman, Adam and Eve, is literally true, or whether it is simply a mythical representation of a certain truth, each person is free to decide for himself. What is accepted by Christians is that the first humans were free from suffering, did not have to experience physical hardship, pain, anxiety, disease or death. By some act of disobedience, by refusing to accept the authority of their creator, they lost these gifts and thus they were lost to all mankind. They lost in addition the gift of divine life and their guilt was incurred by all their descendants. This will only be understood from the Catholic viewpoint when we examine the nature of God's love and see what is meant by grace and the sacraments.

From this first sin, which was called Original Sin, men went on to commit other sins and greater violations of the divine law. Christ's life and suffering was an atonement of these offences, of all offences committed within time by mortal, created beings against an infinite,

William Blake's colour-printed drawing of God judging Adam. The original can be seen in the Tate Gallery.

eternal God. The sufferings of individuals are, in the context of Christ's suffering, beneficial to all mankind and a contribution on the part of man towards this atonement.

Resurrection

The emphasis of Christianity is not on the suffering of Christ and of men, but on the joy of his resurrection from the dead which brings the promise of resurrection from the dead for all men who will then either resume their glorified, transformed bodies and exist in a state of everlasting happiness, or spend all eternity isolated from their God and experiencing the torment of this loss. As a result of their way of life in this world, men will have been responsible, by their own free will, for their own fate: they will have chosen heaven or hell.

Love

We can see how in view of what has just been said, material benefits and the pleasures of this life, together with suffering and death, fall into a position of relative unimportance.

The central point of Christianity is love, or charity. The life of the Christian should be an effort to respond to God's love, and all Christ's teaching and that of his Church are directed towards this end. The test or proof of this love rests in our love for our fellow men. By loving others, we love God; the extent to which we love others determines the degree of our love for God. When Christ enjoined his followers to love others, he was not referring simply to those whom they would love naturally — family, relatives and friends — but to all men, including those who would try to persecute and kill them.

18

Translated into general, practical terms, this means that the Christian
should fulfil his social and family responsibilities while seeking, even
in opposition to his own feelings, to assist his fellow men by good
deeds and by prayer, regardless of differences of belief or nationality,
of opposition or ingratitude.

However, given man's nature, his capacity for self-interest, self-deceit,
and every form of evil, any degree of attainment of this Christian ideal
is impossible without divine assistance. In fact the very nature of love
is divine, and rather than speak of responding to God's love, we should
really be speaking of the love of God, of God Himself making Himself
present within us. The extent to which God is present in a man's soul
is the extent to which that man truly loves — and lives.

The Catholic believes that this love, this divine life, and the assistance
to live as Christ intends, is transmitted to him by grace.

Grace

Grace is a divine gift. Catholic theologians distinguish two kinds:
sanctifying and actual grace. Sanctifying grace is the means whereby
God cleanses the soul of sin, gives to it the supernatural life that was
lost to mankind by our first parents, and grants the power of faith,
of belief in Himself. Actual grace is the strength or power that God
gives to the Christian to overcome temptations and to observe His
commandments.

God conveys His grace to the individual in special ways, mainly
through the seven sacraments which the Catholic Church claims to have
been instituted by Christ during his lifetime, and the practice and
observance of which is borne out by Tradition. They are always, as
we shall see, accompanied by some external sign or ceremony which
must usually be performed by a bishop or priest of the Church.

It should be made clear that the Catholic does not hold that these
are necessarily the only means by which God sanctifies or helps the
individual. There have been many Catholics who have adhered strongly
to the view that if a man, no matter what his professed belief or lack
of belief, honestly and sincerely strives, in the light of his intelligence,
to live as he considers he should, then God will confer grace on that
man's soul, forgive him his sins and grant him a share in His life.

One contemporary Catholic writer speaks of the central character
in one of his novels, an atheist, as having believed without knowing it,
as having loved God without being aware of it. Belief and knowledge
should never be confused. Very often the Catholic himself, like anyone
else, has difficulty in gauging the extent of his belief.

4　The seven sacraments

Baptism

Through Baptism a person's guilt and sharing in the first sin of mankind is removed, he or she receives the gift of divine life and becomes a member of Christ's Church.

The simple rite of Baptism consists of one person pouring water on the head of the person to be baptized while reciting the words: 'I baptize thee in the name of the Father, and of the Son, and of the Holy Spirit.' The ceremony is usually performed by a priest but, in cases of necessity, it may be performed by any person who has attained the age of reason. The Church insists, on account of the absolute necessity of Baptism, that a person be baptized as soon as possible after birth.

At Baptism, there must be at least one godparent, preferably two — a man and a woman, both Catholics — who speak for the child and promise, in the child's name, to live a good Christian life. Should the child's parents die, then they are bound to see that the child is brought up in the Catholic faith.

Some people say that God in His goodness could not allow a baby who dies without Baptism to suffer eternally through no fault of its own, and they use this as an argument against Baptism. It is true that we cannot believe that God would allow a child to suffer in this way, but it is also true that the divine life conferred on our naturally immortal souls by this sacrament is a gift and cannot be merited. Most Catholics think that God provides for such children a state of happiness called Limbo.

There are two substitutes for this sacrament known technically as the 'baptism of blood' and the 'baptism of desire'. The Church teaches that any unbaptized person who dies in defence of his belief in Christ or a Christian virtue receives sanctifying grace and is cleansed of all his sins. Similarly, any person who has not been baptized who performs an act of complete contrition, i.e. sorrow for his sins, and shows great charity, i.e. love of God, likewise receives these benefits.

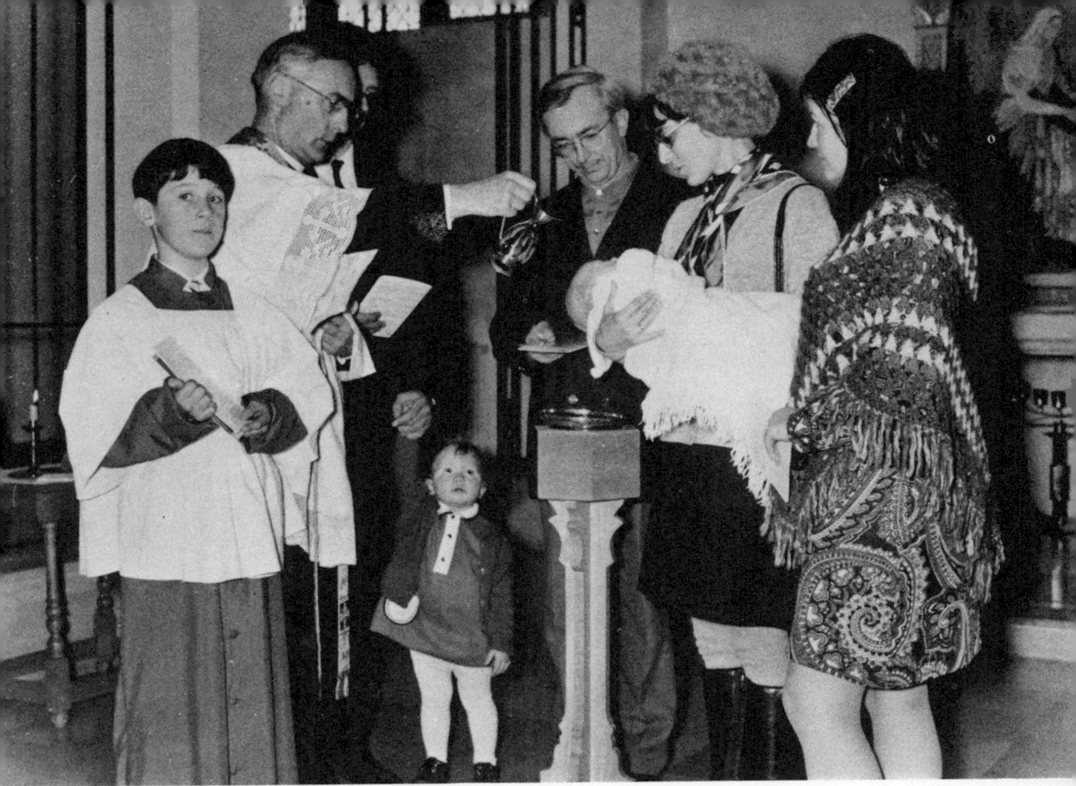

The Baptism ceremony — the godmother holds the baby as the priest pours water on its head.

Confirmation

Confirmation is the sacrament that gives a person the grace to live a Christian life. Whereas Baptism is the sacrament of spiritual birth, Confirmation is the sacrament of spiritual strength, when the Holy Spirit increases its presence in the soul of the person who is confirmed.

Like Baptism this sacrament is conferred only once in a lifetime and then on someone who has already been baptized. It is conferred by a bishop (in special circumstances by a priest) usually after the person has attained the age of reason. The bishop imposes his hands over the person to be confirmed and prays. He then anoints his forehead with chrism (holy oil, the symbol of strength) in the form of a cross, while reciting the words: 'Receive the seal of the gift of the Holy Spirit.'

It is the custom for children to take another first name, that of a saint, when they are confirmed. They are encouraged to choose a saint whom they admire and to whose life they can look for inspiration and example.

The bishop makes the sign of the cross upon the forehead of the person being confirmed. The godparent stands behind with his right hand upon the candidate's shoulder.

The Blessed Eucharist

The word 'Eucharist' means 'thanksgiving' and is the name given to the wonderful act that Christ performed on the eve of his death when he was at supper with the Apostles. During the course of this meal he took bread, blessed it and broke it, saying: 'Take ye, and eat: this is my body.' After the meal was ended he took a cup of wine which he gave to them, saying: 'Drink ye all of this, for this is my blood of the New Testament which shall be shed for many unto remissions of sins ' (Matthew 26: 26-28).

Many Christians maintain that Christ, on this as on other occasions when he spoke of eating his flesh and drinking his blood, was speaking figuratively and did not wish to be taken literally. The Catholic, however, believes that a great change really took place, that without the bread and wine changing in taste or appearance, Christ was giving himself to his followers, was uniting himself to them not only spiritually but physically. The power of performing this rite was to be given to the Apostles and transmitted by them to their successors so that all who believed in Christ could be brought closer to him and to one another.

Only bishops and priests can consecrate bread and wine, as this action is called, and they do so during the ceremony of the Mass which we shall be considering in the next chapter and which

The tabernacle, which stands in the centre of the altar, must be covered when it contains the Blessed Sacrament.

is the sacrament of which the Eucharist forms the central part. After the Consecration members of the congregation may approach the altar and receive Communion, i.e. partake of the body of Christ by eating the consecrated bread. The actual transformation of the bread and wine into the body and blood of Christ is known as Transubstantiation.

Not all the consecrated bread is consumed at Mass; some is kept locked in a container on the altar and a light is kept burning to indicate Christ's real presence. This sacrament is also called the Blessed Sacrament.

Catholics usually start receiving Communion around the age of seven.

One of the altar boys receives Communion from the priest.

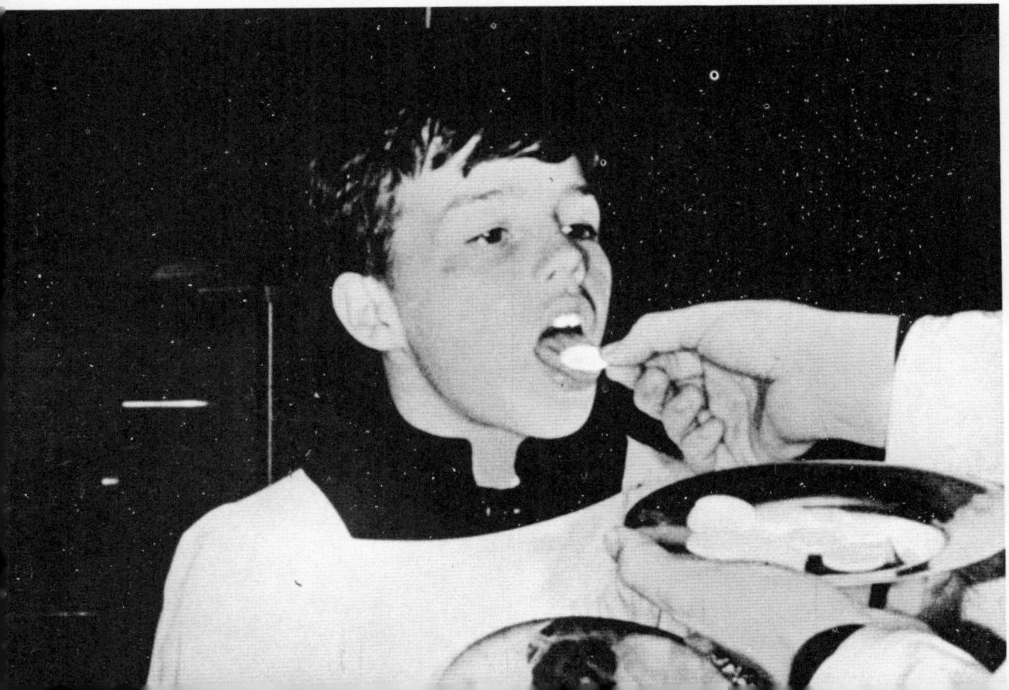

Penance

If a Catholic has committed any serious sin since he last received
Communion, he must first receive the sacrament of Penance
before he can again receive Communion.

The Church teaches that the sacrament of Penance was instituted
by Christ for the forgiveness of sins committed after Baptism. This
grace of forgiveness is transmitted through the bishops and priests of
the Church. It is God, not they, who forgives; their task is simply to
act as mediators and pronounce the words of forgiveness.
Absolution (the grace of forgiveness) is withheld if certain
conditions are not fulfilled.

This sacrament may be received anywhere, but the usual procedure
is for the Catholic who wishes to receive the sacrament to go to a
Catholic church at the time advertised for the hearing of confessions.
A cubicle, normally divided into two parts, is provided for the purpose
and is to be found usually at the side of the church. One part is
occupied by the priest and a small grill in the partition wall allows
him to speak with the person receiving the sacrament, known as the
penitent, who occupies the other part.

Separated from
each other by a
grill, the priest
hears the
penitent's
Confession.

Contrition

The penitent must first make an Act of Contrition. This means that
he must express, usually in the form of a set prayer, his sincere
sorrow at having offended his creator. He must be sorry but without
necessarily feeling sorry; clearly it is very difficult to feel sorry for an
act that gave one a great deal of pleasure, but one can recognize its
wrongness and regret it.

Confession

The penitent must next specify any serious (mortal) sin committed
since his last Confession. He may also, but is under no compulsion to
do so, mention any lesser (venial) sins that he has committed.

If a Catholic has committed a mortal sin, he has cut himself off
from the life of the Church, received through Baptism, and
readmission is normally through the sacrament of Penance. It
would be wrong, however, to assume that this sacrament is reserved
only for those who have fallen into serious sin. Very many
Catholics make a practice of confessing their sins once a month or
even at more frequent intervals, to obtain the increase of grace that
this sacrament affords. If they have committed no serious sins, then
they confess their lesser ones; if there are no sins to confess, then
they say so and express their sorrow for past sins.

A priest is bound, even at the cost of his life, not to disclose
anything he learns from a person's Confession. When he himself
wishes to receive the sacrament he will go to another priest, in the
way that any other penitent does.

Satisfaction

Before pronouncing the words of absolution, the priest imposes a
penance. It is not sufficient for the penitent to be sorry for his sins;
he must in some way make up for them. The penance usually consists
of the recitation of certain prayers.

The debt of temporal punishment as it is called, this necessity to
make up for one's sins, is, unless the sorrow of the penitent is
so completely perfect and adequate, only partially removed by the
penance imposed by the priest. This debt can be removed either by
voluntary suffering or by gaining Indulgences in this life, or in the
next life by the pains of purgatory which is the intermediate state
between heaven and hell.

Indulgences

Perhaps no part of Catholic teaching has been more criticized and

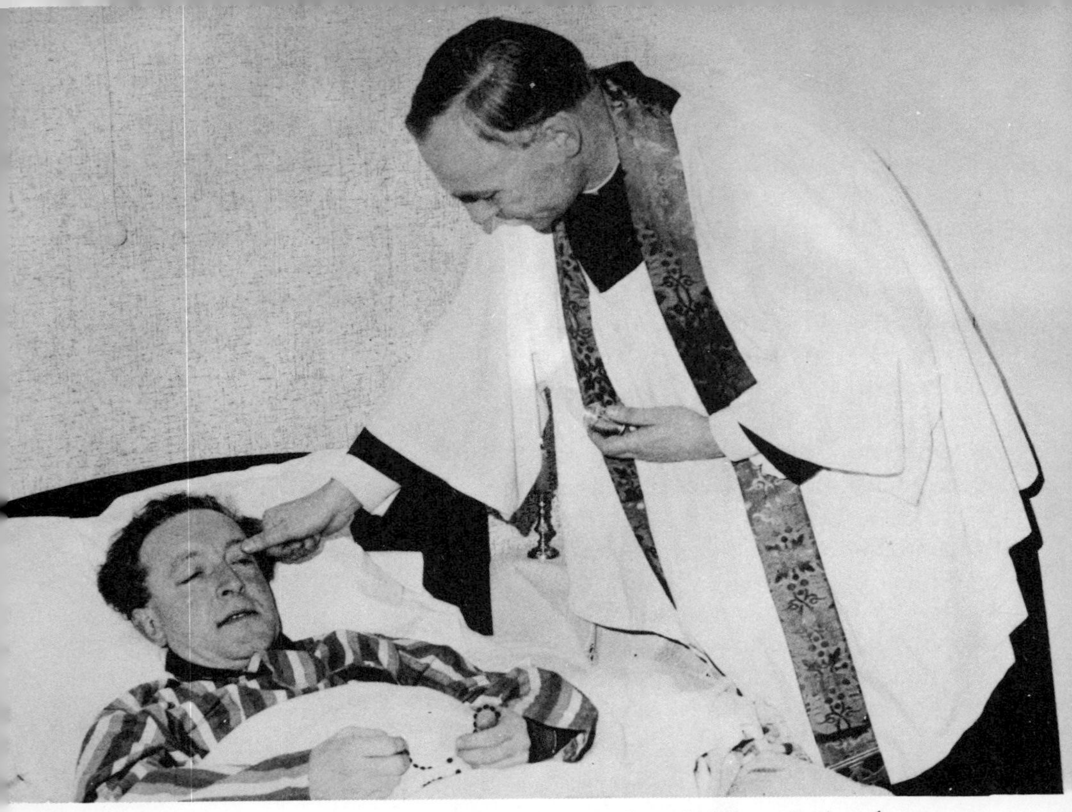

The priest anoints the forehead of the sick man who is holding a Rosary (see page 42).

more misunderstood than that concerning Indulgences. An Indulgence is not a pardon of sin, still less is it a permission to commit sin; it is a release from temporal punishment granted by the Church, outside the sacrament of Penance.

Historically, Indulgences may roughly be divided into ancient and modern: the ancient extending over the first twelve centuries, the modern from about the end of the thirteenth century to the present day. The ancient Indulgences were only granted to penitents who had been guilty of serious sin, and who were thus enabled to satisfy God's justice by prayers, the giving of alms and pilgrimages. Modern Indulgences are of wider application, being offered to all who are liable for any debt of temporal punishment. These Indulgences may be either plenary (remitting the whole of the temporal debt) or partial (remitting only a part). Conditions for obtaining an Indulgence are specifically laid down by the Church. Indulgences are granted by the Holy Father and, under certain restrictions, by bishops.

The anointing of the sick

This is the sacrament through which those in danger of death from
sickness or old age receive grace for their spiritual strength and comfort,
and sometimes too divine assistance by which they are restored to health.
This sacrament also takes away small (venial) sins, and it also forgives the
serious (mortal) sins of people too ill to make a confession of these sins.

The sacrament is administered by a priest who anoints the sick
person on the forehead and on the hands, saying: 'Through this holy
anointing and because of his great love for us, may the Lord fill you with
the power of his Holy Spirit. May he also take your sins away and give
you salvation and strength.'

Although there are cases, as medical experience attests, where people
who are gravely ill have made remarkable recoveries after receiving this
sacrament, its healing power is not necessarily miraculous. If a person
is in an untroubled state of mind then his body usually has more chance
of recovery than if he is tormented by fear or wrong. It is therefore in
the patient's physical, as well as spiritual, interests that a priest be
summoned even if there is only a very slight danger of death.

The marriage
service takes
place in church.
The wedding ring
is blessed by the
priest and the
bridegroom then
places it on the
ring finger of the
bride's left hand.

Matrimony

Matrimony is the sacrament which unites a Christian man and a
Christian woman, whether Catholic or non-Catholic, as husband and
wife, and gives them the grace to fulfil their duties in the married
state. It is a binding agreement by which two baptized persons
undertake to live faithfully together as husband and wife from that
moment forward until parted by death, and to bring up their children
in the Catholic faith.

A Catholic marriage usually takes place in a Catholic church in the
presence of a priest. The priest is there as a witness to the marriage,
as the Church's official representative. It is not through him that
grace is transmitted, but through the partners of the marriage by
their mutual giving and acceptance.

Divorce

In obedience to Christ's command, divorce is not permitted by the
Catholic Church. If, however, certain essential conditions of a
marriage are found not to have been fulfilled, for example if there
are no witnesses or if the bride gave her consent through fear then
the marriage can be declared to have been invalid. The Church may
also grant a separation between a husband and wife, but both partners
are still bound by their promise of faithfulness and neither may
contract another marriage while the other is alive.

Mixed marriages

A marriage between a Catholic and a non-Catholic requires the
permission of a bishop. This can only be granted if the non-Catholic
partner undertakes not to impede the other's practice of his or her
faith, and to allow any children of the marriage to be brought up as
Catholics.

The Church discourages mixed marriages for a number of reasons,
perhaps the strongest being that in practice they are not always a
success. Many non-Catholics agree to abide by the conditions
mentioned above without fully realizing how much being married to
a Catholic will affect their whole lives. All too frequently couples of
mixed marriages find themselves in disagreement on certain important
issues, for example over the use of artificial methods of birth control,
or over the kind of schooling their children should receive. From the
point of view of the children, it will be at the least disturbing to
realize that only one parent is practising the religion to which they
themselves are being taught to attach so much importance.

Holy Order

Holy Order is the sacrament which imparts to a man the gift of the
Holy Spirit so that he can perform validly and worthily the duties of
deacon, priest or bishop. The sacrament therefore can be conferred
in three degrees.

We know from the New Testament that the Apostles appointed
helpers and successors. We read of the first deacons that seven men
of 'good reputation, full of the Holy Ghost and wisdom' were chosen;
that they were 'set before the Apostles' who 'praying imposed hands
upon them' (Acts 6: 3-6).

Only a bishop may administer the Holy Order, only he may 'ordain'
another bishop, a priest or a deacon. He does so by the laying on of
hands, by placing his hands on the head of the man being ordained,

The bishop ordains the
priest by the laying on
of hands.

and by reciting certain prayers. The laying on of hands (cf
Confirmation) shows that some kind of power is being given; the
words of the prayer show that it is a sacred or holy power. No
woman, in obedience to the command of Christ, is allowed to
receive this sacrament.

The clergy

Bishops, priests and deacons, considered as a body, are known as the
clergy; all other Catholics are referred to as the laity.

The deacon receives the power of preaching effectively and of
baptizing, and of worthily and reverently assisting the priest and
the bishop at the sacrifice of the Mass. The priest, who is also a
deacon, receives the power of forgiving sin and of offering the
sacrifice of the Mass. The bishop receives the power of
confirming and ordaining. It is through the bishops, therefore,
that the power bestowed by Christ on his Apostles to consecrate
the Blessed Eucharist, to absolve from sin, to confirm, and to
give the Holy Unction to the sick, is always kept alive in the
Church. Every bishop is also a priest.

In addition to these spiritual powers, the bishop has the authority
to teach and to govern. As we saw earlier, the bishops, with the Pope
as their head and as the legitimate successors of the Apostles,
constitute the governing body of the Church.

Without bishops there would be no Church; although
theoretically there need not be priests or deacons as such, it
would be hard to imagine the Church existing without them.

The celibacy of the clergy

All members of the clergy are bound by a vow of chastity. The
celibacy of the clergy was instituted by the Church and it is within
the power of the Pope to repeal this law. It was generally observed
during the first three centuries, and was imposed as a law about the
year 400 AD.

In view of the work and duties of the clergy, there are obvious
reasons for the existence of this law. A man without a family is able
to give himself completely to his work; he is not distracted by family
affections and cares. People are more likely to entrust their secrets
in confession to a man who has no intimate ties and that man is more
able to retain those secrets if he has none.

There are people who, without necessarily disputing the value of
celibacy, have serious misgivings about its possibility. How, they ask,
can a man live without any kind of sex life without becoming

frustrated, over tense, perhaps warped in his outlook, even bitter or
perverted? Naturally speaking, the suppression of such a basic human
appetite will tend to lead to such disorders, but if we accept the
reality of grace then the exclusion of all sexual activity from a man's
life, while remaining difficult, is none the less placed distinctly within
his capacity. The normalcy of the vast majority of priests is probably
one of the greatest proofs of God's grace. It does not necessarily
follow that because a man is celibate, he is not able to understand
sexual problems; the very great struggle to remain celibate in itself
produces understanding and sympathy for problems of this kind.
Moreover, from listening to Confessions, priests obtain a greater
insight into human nature and human problems than most people.
We are now at a time when, after a period of more than fifteen
hundred years, there is a distinct possibility that there will be a
relaxation of this law and, should this transpire, it will be interesting
to see how many members of the clergy will avail themselves of the
opportunity to marry and how their work will compare with that of
unmarried members.

Religious Orders
Within the Church there are many communities of men and women
who bind themselves to lead a life devoted entirely to some Christian
work. They may, for example, devote their lives primarily to prayer,
fasting and penance, as with the Carthusians, or to preaching and
education, as with the Jesuits, or to nursing, as with the Sisters of St
Vincent de Paul. In common with the priest, they take a vow of
chastity and sometimes, depending on the Order, take additional vows
such as those of poverty or obedience. One can usually distinguish
the Order to which they belong by their mode of dress.

A member of a Religious Order as such does not receive the
sacrament of Holy Order, although a man may be both a priest and a
Religious i.e. belong to an Order.

5   The way Catholics worship

The sacrifice of the Mass
To treat the Mass in full would require a book in itself and one considerably greater in length than this. It is only possible here to give the briefest of outlines of what the Mass is and try to indicate why it should occupy a position of supreme importance in the life of the Catholic.

We have already seen, in a very brief treatment of the Blessed Eucharist, that the Consecration constitutes the central part of the Mass and that it is followed by Communion. The Mass, however, signifies far more than the changing of bread and wine into the body and blood of Christ and the partaking of his body by those present who so desire. The Mass is first and foremost a sacrifice.

There are a number of reasons why men offer public sacrifices to God: they do so as a sign that they love Him and honour Him, as an expression of their gratitude and repentance, but primarily and originally they do so in an attempt to obtain forgiveness for their sins. They offer Him something which is of value to them and which they believe will be acceptable to Him. From the Old Testament we learn that God laid down forms of sacrifice to be observed by His chosen people, the Jews, and told them who were to be their priests i.e. those who were to offer the sacrifice on their behalf. The gift, or victim as it was called, to be offered was usually an animal such as a lamb or an ox which to these tribal people were among their most valued possessions. The killing of these animals symbolized their being given completely to God.

These sacrifices were a preparation, a gradual working towards the supreme sacrifice to be made by Christ. Many of them were unacceptable to God as they were not made out of love or any of the dispositions we have already mentioned; and none of them could achieve what ultimately they were intended for, namely God's forgiveness. No offering however great, even that of a person's life, could make up for man's sins. Man of himself could not reach God. God alone was able to bridge the gulf that existed between Himself

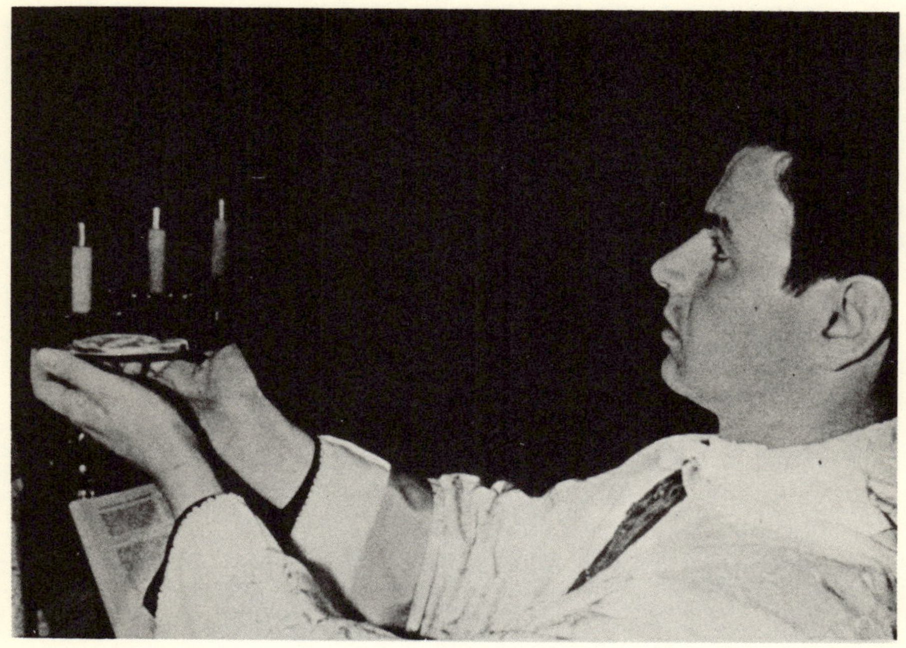

At Mass the priest offers the bread saying, 'Blessed are you, Lord, God of all creation. Through your goodness we have this bread to offer, which earth has given and human hands have made. It will become for us the bread of life.'

He then offers the chalice containing the wine saying, 'Blessed are you, Lord, God of all creation. Through your goodness we have this wine to offer, fruit of the vine and work of human hands. It will become our spiritual drink.'

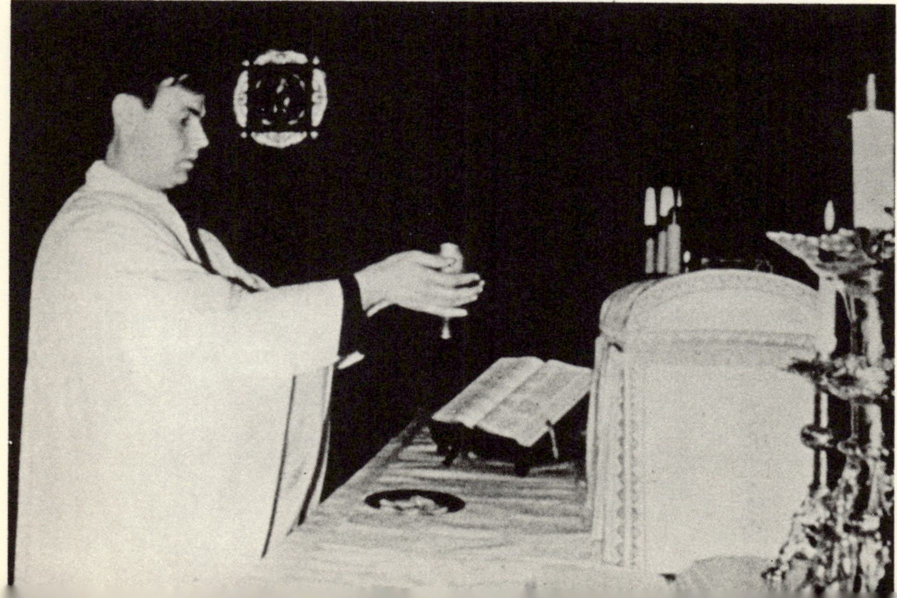

and man. He did so by sending His son, by coming on earth Himself
and offering Himself as a victim. When Christ allowed himself to be
nailed to the cross on Mount Calvary outside the walls of Jerusalem,
he was, as priest and victim, offering himself to God in atonement for
the sins of mankind.

Christ, on the night before he died, gave this sacrifice to his Apostles
so that they too could offer it. He made it their sacrifice as well and
that of all who should believe in him. The Mass is not merely a memorial
service, a simple commemoration of Christ's sacrifice; it is a bloodless
re-enaction, a real continuation within time of the sacrifice of Calvary,
when Christ at the altar offers himself to the Father on behalf of all
members of the Church, living and dead. The real priest is still Christ; the
man standing at the altar is the person through whom God works — he
and all those present join with Christ in offering their great gift to God.
Those who attend Mass with the right dispositions derive all the grace
that they need in their everyday lives and obtain grace for all those who
believe in Him.

**In many Catholic churches the priest now stands behind the altar and faces the
congregation during Mass. On one side are the two altar boys who assist him.**

The priest breaks the consecrated bread in two. He then takes Communion himself before serving it to the congregation.

In the light of this one public sacrifice, all other private sacrifices made by Catholics have a value if made for the right reasons. Even in small ways, such as by refraining from eating certain things that they like, or by getting up early when they would prefer to lie in bed, Catholics can make offerings to God that have been made acceptable by the sacrifice of Christ and which will bring an increase in grace.

The Mass begins with an introduction of prayers, readings from the Scriptures and usually a sermon delivered by the priest. This is followed by the Creed, a profession of Catholic belief recited by all present, and other prayers. The actual Mass now begins and consists of the Offertory, the Consecration and the Communion. During the Offertory, the people can bring their own offerings to the altar and join with the priest in offering themselves and their gifts, together with Christ, to God.

The Mass may vary considerably in length and form, depending on the introduction and additional ceremonial, but it always consists basically of the Offertory, Consecration and Communion. A simple Mass may last no more than half an hour, but a more solemn Mass when several priests say Mass together (concelebration) and when much of the service is sung, will last considerably longer. Mass is said in many Catholic churches on every day of the year.

All Catholics are bound to attend Mass every Sunday unless circumstances prevent them from doing so. They must also receive Communion at least once a year during a specified period.

The Liturgy

The word 'Liturgy' means 'public service'. During the course of a
year, the Church, in the readings from the Scriptures and the prayers
at Mass, though the sermons of the priests and by means of additional
ceremonies, re-enacts the entire life of Christ from the period prior to
his birth until his rising up into heaven. Christ's teaching and his life
are put before the Catholic to be observed and to be emulated. He is
called upon to share in Christ's joys and sufferings and to identify
them as far as possible with his own. Everything about the Liturgy,
from the colour of the clothes (vestments) worn by the priest to the
texts read from the Scriptures are intended as aids towards this end.

The Church year begins with Advent. The word 'Advent' means
'coming' and for a few weeks before Christmas the Church prepares
for the coming of Christ by reminding Catholics of their need to do
penance, to be sorry for their sins and to recognize their complete
unworthiness to receive him. Christmas is the birthday of Christ,
the Son of God, who came on earth to forgive men their sins and offer
them a share in His life. After Christmas we are further reminded of
the infancy of Christ by the feast of the Epiphany, which
commemorates the visit of the Magi, the wise men from the East who
came to pay homage to him, and the feast of the Holy Family, of the child
Jesus together with his mother Mary, and his stepfather Joseph.

A few weeks after this, usually some time in February, begins the
penitential season, Lent, when the Church encourages its members to
make private sacrifices and to deny themselves some of this world's
comforts. For forty days the Church unfolds the story of man's
salvation and the services, which include many of the prophecies of
the Old Testament, are a gradual preparation for the suffering and
death of Christ.

Easter Sunday is the greatest feast in the Church's calendar.
It is the day of Christ's resurrection, the proof of his divinity,
and the promise of future happiness. The lights, flowers and music
contrast violently with the bareness, the silence and the emptiness
of the previous two days, Good Friday and Holy Saturday. Forty days
after Easter the Church celebrates the Ascension, when Christ in his
transfigured, glorified body left his Apostles and returned to heaven.
Ten days later comes Pentecost — the Greek word for 'fifty' because
Pentecost is fifty days after Easter. This is the day of the Confirmation
of the Apostles when they received the gift of the Holy Spirit and
when the Church was really born. Pentecost was once a favourite
feast for the Baptism of new Christians and, as they wore white

garments, this feast has also come to be called Whit Sunday. Two other great feasts follow soon afterwards, Corpus Christi, when Catholics celebrate Christ's real presence still among them, and the Sacred Heart, when they honour the great love of their Saviour. During the summer and autumn the Liturgy is comparatively uneventful; the three years of Christ's public life are put before Catholics and, through his teaching and miracles, they are reminded of their everyday duties.

In the course of the year, in addition to Sundays, there are several days, usually six or seven in number but varying to some extent from one country to another, when Catholics are bound to attend Mass. They are known as Holy Days of Obligation.

Until recently, all adult Catholics in good health were required to abstain from eating meat on Fridays as a penance and as a reminder that this was the day of Christ's death. There now only remain, in England at least, two days of abstinence — Ash Wednesday, the first day of Lent, and Good Friday. These two days are also the only two remaining days of fasting. Fasting does not mean, as it does in some other religions, that Catholics must refrain from eating altogether, but their meals are limited by certain stringent regulations, the details of which every Catholic should know. At one time there were very many fast days, particularly during Lent. Now, for a number of reasons, perhaps not least being the need to keep physically abreast of the pace of modern life, these have been abolished. Fasting and abstinence days, like Holy Days of Obligation, vary from one country to another, depending largely on custom and the instructions of bishops.

Prayer

Prayer in the widest sense is the most essential element of any religion — it really means the same thing as religion. Every religious practice and every action of a person performed in the belief that it is in accordance with God's wishes constitutes a prayer. The very life of a person, when given entirely to God's service, is a prayer.

Very often, however, the meaning of prayer is restricted to verbal communication with God: it may be in public, sung, spoken or chanted according to a fixed pattern of words, when a community gather together to worship God; it may be in private when an individual addresses his creator either according to these set forms or spontaneously in his own words, aloud or in silence.

In the Catholic Church there are many set prayers, largely composed by saints or taken from the Bible, which are chosen for their beauty and their content, expressing more perfectly than

ordinary Catholics can their religious sentiments and ideas. The two
prayers of this kind most commonly used are the 'Our Father' and the
'Hail Mary'. The 'Our Father' was the prayer given by Christ to his
Apostles and, with very minor differences, is that adopted by all
Christians. The 'Hail Mary' is the prayer most often used by Catholics
when addressing the mother of Christ, the main part of which consists
of two texts from the New Testament, the words of greeting used by
the heavenly messenger sent to announce to Mary that she was to become
the mother of Christ, and those used to greet her by her cousin
Elizabeth whom she went to visit shortly afterwards.

For Catholics prayer is a source of actual grace, and they have
always been encouraged by the Church to pray in private as well as
in public, at all times to communicate their thoughts and troubles to
God and to remind themselves of His presence and of their relationship
to Him. Unlike most other Christians however, Catholics do not pray
simply to God, the Father, the Son or the Holy Spirit, but also the
saints, to those whom they believe to be already united to God in
heaven, and primarily to the Blessed Virgin Mary.

The sight of a Catholic kneeling before the statue of a saint has
sometimes given rise to the belief that he is worshipping the saint, or
even that he is worshipping the statue. Statues, like many other
things used in Catholic worship, are an aid to concentration; they
help focus the attention and exclude irrelevant thoughts. Catholics
in no way worship statues, nor do they worship saints in the strict
sense of the word; only God is truly worshipped. The word 'worship'
however can mean 'honour', and Catholics do hold in great honour
those who are already in heaven and believe in enlisting their support
when they have a particular request to make. The prayer of petition
is probably the most frequent kind of prayer in any religion. When a
Catholic asks a saint to pray on his behalf, this is known as
'intercession' – the Saint intercedes between the person and God.
Why not, one might well ask, pray to God directly? The answer to
this rests mainly in the belief that the closer a person is to God, the
more effective is his prayer. This is why Catholics pray so frequently
to the Blessed Virgin, because she is closer to God than any of the
saints and many believe that when she does intercede on their behalf
no request of hers is refused.

The angels

Before we consider the unique position held by Mary in Catholic
worship, a word should be said of those often much neglected
spiritual beings, the angels, to whom Catholics are also encouraged to

pray. The Church teaches that angels were created by God before the
beginning of the world and that they were put through some kind of
test whereby they were free to choose the love of God or reject it.
Those who chose the former course, like Michael and Gabriel, are
sent to help mankind; those like Lucifer (or Satan as he was later
called) who rebelled against God, try to set men against God and
encourage them to every form of evil. Although there is much doubt,
even among Christians, regarding the existence of Satan (also called
the Devil) and his followers, it would appear direct contact with
him has been by no means uncommon among Christians and
non-Christians alike.

The Blessed Virgin Mary
Catholics honour Mary as the only person pure enough to fulfil the
greatest responsibility and to receive the greatest blessing ever given to
a human being.

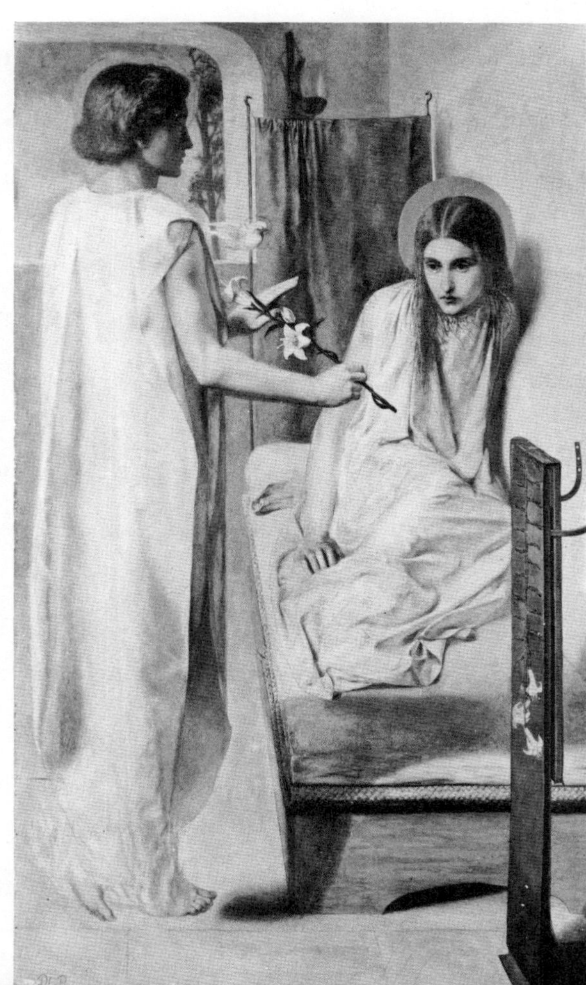

The angel tells Mary she
will be the mother of
Christ. (The Annunciation
by Dante Gabriel Rossetti.)

The angel sent to inform her of her mission greeted her with the
words: 'Hail, full of grace.' Mary, as the mother of the son of
God, was completely sinless. She was conceived without a share
in original sin and this is what Catholics mean when they say
that they believe in the Immaculate Conception. This part
of Catholic teaching must not be confused with the virgin birth, when
Mary gave birth to Jesus not as the result of any physical relationship
with man but from the direct action of the Holy Spirit.

One of the penalties of original sin, as we saw in the first chapter,
was death, the separation of body and soul and the disintegration of
the human body, but Catholics believe that Mary, alone of all mortals,
when the time came for her to leave this world, was united body and
soul with her son in heaven. This is the teaching of the Assumption.

Most Catholics possess a circle of beads known as a Rosary. It is by
reciting prayers, nearly all of which are Hail Marys, one for each bead,
that they most commonly pray to Mary.

**The Cathedral of Christ the King in Liverpool. One of the most modern Roman
Catholic cathedrals in Britain, it was opened in 1967.**

The interior of the Church of the Holy Ghost in Balham, showing the fine stained glass window over the altar. The tabernacle can be seen in the middle of the altar, in front of the crucifix.

Churches

Members of most religions have a meeting place where they gather to worship. But where Catholics are concerned, a church is more than simply a place of worship — it houses the Blessed Sacrament, it is the place where God is really, physically present in the body of His Son Jesus Christ. This explains why in Catholic churches silence is closely observed and why there is a great display of reverence. It will also explain why Catholics devote so much effort and money to building beautiful churches.

Devotional practices

In addition to the Mass and the other ceremonies of the Liturgy,
there are many religious services and practices which, without forming
a fundamental part of Catholic teaching, can nevertheless be a source
of actual grace for those who attend or observe them. Some of these,
like the Rosary, have been in existence for hundreds of years and are
to be found universally; others are of lesser standing and more limited
range. Because there are so many it would be impossible to mention
all of them here, so we will take a brief look at some of the most
common.

On entering a Catholic church, one will usually see around the
walls fourteen tableaux depicting the last sufferings, death and burial
of Christ. These are known as the Stations of the Cross. It is the
custom throughout Lent to join with the priest in praying and
thinking about these experiences of Christ. The priest, together with
the altar servers, those boys or men who assist him in the performance
of church ceremonies, will spend a few minutes in front of each
tableau, while the congregation turn in their direction.

Benediction is held in many churches on occasions. This is a short
service when the Blessed Eucharist which is kept in the tabernacle,
the container on the altar, is taken out for worship.

Catholics frequently make pilgrimages. They will travel to some
holy place, very often the place where a saint lived and worked,
to pray and do penance. Sometimes the actual journey is made
very arduous and difficult.

Jesus, carrying his cross to Calvary,
meets Mary his mother. The fourth
of the Fourteen Stations of the Cross.

Pilgrims praying at Lourdes, in south-west France. The statue marks the place where the Virgin Mary first appeared in 1858 to Bernadette Soubirous, who became Saint Bernadette in 1933.

From time to time, Retreats are held in a church, which all Catholics living in the area are encouraged to attend. For a few days, usually a week, one or two visiting priests will preach each night reminding the congregation of their duties and endeavouring to restore them to a more fervent practice of their religion. There are Retreat houses to which Catholics can go for a few days and shut out all the distractions of the outside world while making a Retreat.

Devotional practices include not only public services or practices of this kind, but a whole host of simple actions such as making the sign of the cross, sprinkling something with holy water, going down on one knee whenever passing in front of the Blessed Eucharist, kneeling while praying, kissing a Rosary, lighting a candle before a statue, all of which have a simple significance which is usually self-evident.

Sometimes non-Catholics point to the many divergences of opinion within the Catholic Church and infer disunity. It would be a mistake to consider that a Catholic is bound within a straightjacket of dogma. Religion is essentially a personal matter and different attitudes, different views can be held relating to many aspects of the faith. Even fundamental beliefs can be regarded in different ways and frequently form the subject of discussion among Catholics. The true Catholic does not blindly acquiesce; he seeks humbly to accept and, as far as possible, to understand.

Suggestions for further reading

The Bible: Revised Standard Version (Fontana 1966)
F. H. Drinkwater *Telling the Good News* (Macmillan and Burns and Oates 1960)
F. J. Somerville *Religious Textbooks for Catholic Grammar Schools Series* (Nelson 1958/62)
F. J. Sheed *Faith Comes by Hearing* (Stag Books, Sheed and Ward 1967)

The Catholic Truth Society, 38/40 Eccleston Square, London SW 1, publish inexpensive pamphlets dealing with various aspects of Catholic belief and practice.

Index